(un)interru

Dal(binde

for Jess

♡ Dal x

In wild solidarity...

First published 19th August 2022 by Fly on the Wall Press
Published in the UK by
Fly on the Wall Press
56 High Lea Rd
New Mills
Derbyshire
SK22 3DP

www.flyonthewallpress.co.uk
ISBN:9781913211820

Typesetting by Isabelle Kenyon. Cover Illustrator - Natalie Leyland.

A CIP Catalogue record for this book is available from the British Library.

Author's Note:

All instances of language, spelling and punctuation throughout this chapbook are deliberate acts of finding a language that meets my experiences as a Brown woman and are deliberately anti-literary.

time(less) li(n)e

Ancestors ~ way-back

|

Anglo-Indian War | 1857

|

Partition of India | 1947

|

SS Kular arrives in Birmingham | 1954

|

SS Kular & R Kaur arrive in Sheffield | 1959

|

Dalbinder Kaur Kular born in Sheffield | 1968

|

Margaret Thatcher becomes Prime Minister | 1979

|

Last breath, left palm ~ Sheffield | 2016

|

Ancestor speaks me | 2019

this work is a

MEsS.

My m-

ess.

Every s p

i

ll -a

G

e

&

spell

mS*take|

I own it alL.

What a privilEge it is

to bE (here)

anyway|

white pages| 1974

i was creative before i knew i was brown| i created myself female before i was born| that was my first act of creation| & my first act of defiance| my soul is shades of everything| when i was six i wrote about snow-white-men in royal blue ink across off-

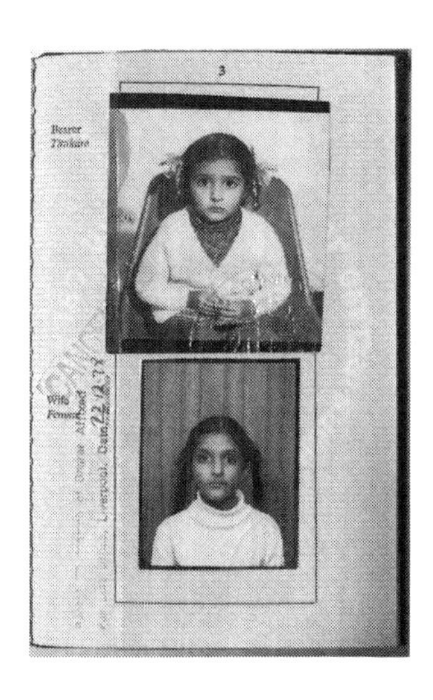

unemploy me from
urban existence|
this colourised land-no-escape||

replant me in the desert,
bone-infested junk yard
of my ever distant
psyche||

pick bones from dust|
Kujichagulia

"...the decision to define ourselves,
name ourselves,
and speak for ourselves,
instead of being
defined and spoken for by
others." Audré Lorde

cleansed|
made virtuous|
by the power of
this work more than by any
Other||

Haunting |ancestor speaks me| Punjab 185?

my tongue was swollen & golden tipped by my sacred longs i

was free & i rolled my life around my mouth & made

scripturised songs learnt to split lines lived in moon-moments

& danced with dandi / dodandi & this is what i say to you

inherited and ancestral wildness|

something greater than

lived by the land

by the wits

at the will of

possibility

myth & wild

planets, seasons & earth,

mysticism, the stars,

gurus and holy men.

wild by folklore,

made of places|

angrez shouts the night alight:

Burn books.

Shut schools.

Interrupt tongues.

Sacred songs.

Unmake this place.

Colourised landscape.

Break will.

Split stars.

The seasons too.

Kill this wild.

Bury songs.

Shut books.

Burn tongues.

Interrupt schools.

Steal planets.

Flatten this land.

Eradicate myth.

Un-holy the folk.

uprise |ancestor speaks me| Sheffield 2019

she whispers in my bones twists my spine with stories sends
shooting stars down my legs until i shakeawake &

listen:

they think they did
it /burned and
buried us too deep
enough to survive
fools/ they fools
where do you think
the song-tongues
go into bones to
ashes to dust to
earth make fresh
flesh tongue-songs
beat heart into life|
uprise & up i
rise. into her bones
her breath
an i into I|
see fire in my eyes
scars on your tongue
i am alive|
made of places
wilded by
others
other-wised by
wild|

Nether Green Middle School

Child's Name. Dalbinder Kular.   Class M1F | **Sheffield 1978**

Teacher's Report

Dalbinder has made excellent progress this year. She has worked steadily and conscientiously. She has settled well into the middle school. Her attitude to work is mature and sensible. Her work in all aspects of English is very good. Her spelling is excellent and her writing is neat and legible. She uses words imaginatively and can write a well-rounded story. She reads well and her comprehension is good. She makes good use of the class and school library.

She is making steady progress in maths, assimilates new work easily and is careful, neat and accurate. She likes thematic work and is capable of finding and recording er own information. She willingly contributes to class discussion.

Dalbinder has taken to French with enthusiasm and is always ready to answer questions. She likes art and craft and is quite creative if somewhat lacking in confidence. She prefers the work to be structured. She is making quite good progress with her recorder and is a very good and keen singer. She is less enthusiastic about physical activities, although she joins in, and seems to enjoy, sports and games.

In class Dalbinder is always friendly and helpful.She has plenty of friends. She seems well set to go forward to an equally successful second year.

(Bruised | 1984 Sheffield.
Ghost of We *(after Ka Ba, Amiri Baraka)*

The Ghost of I looks down into the school yard - all the white kids are walking west. Defying physics. One Brown Girl walks East. Trailing her scream behind her tangled into broken peacock feathers. When the school yard is empty she sucks up the space and spreads her feathers and lets the scream escape into smog.

(I catches it and swallow it whole)

Her world is full of suffocated teal, fuschia and violet, feather tips that stroke the moon, rose incense and gold trim. Muskier than the West walkers. Infused with cardamon pod and clove 1000 eyes that hold the imagineering of Sadhus, Sufis, Sikhs, henna'd hands, jade(d) plains of emerald and Simran.

Yet her soul thrusted West via Pan Am and Satnam (Wahe Guru) into steelscapes, Thatcher and McCains Cheesy deep fried pancakes. She chants 'I'm Going Underground' while her Dada chants the Higher Ground (Satnam Satnam Wahe Guru Satnam...) whilst the white kids live overground.

Her feathers shiver tight. Close In.

She needs the sacred word now, the one that keeps her feathers open like the ancient prayers woven into the ramala so she can hear the Nitnem from her ancestors and the jadoo that will raise her up. The Ghost of I looks down into an empty school yard. One Brown Girl. Plucks her own feathers. One by One.

Each scream slips through I's grasping hands.

A tear drop falls from I's eye. She catches it on her finger tip, looks into it and sees the Ghost of We. We stir magic into each other's eyes. Defiant, she steals the wind and thrusts her remaining feathers open.

She looks west and walks her East into it.

Pure Chana Dal

cooked

Stirring all kinds of influences, new and old, into vital live

FREE FROM PRESERVATIVES
AND ADDITIVES
Do not allow flour to become damp.
Store in a cool dry place and never mix old and new flour

Culture's origins

Specially packed for
East End Foods plc
Kenrick Way,
West Browmwich, B71 4EA
Tel: -44 (0)121 553 1999

A sizeable helping of

Yorkshire pudding

Nonlinearity and time and place

beating heart

soul

BELIEVING |FREE FROM PRESERVATIVES
AND ADDITIVES

Timecircles

Memories

Future Present

Obscure corners

FOR YOU |never mix old and new flour|

What's out there?

Orkney | 2019

Race is the least interesting lie of me. It
visibilises me and invisibilises me in equal
measure. I prefers being invisible on her own
terms. Like the way the North Sea sculpts
the space between the old man and
mainland, splitting sunsets in two.

I is tired of the same old story. You never
see the other part, the wild part, the part
that paradiddles bones, soul dancing by no-
light of dark moons.

She's way more dangerous and free, in the
arms of samurai and skulls. Sometimes she
gets lost in the cloud of forgetting,
becomes an invisible veil like that final
breath gifting a palm, waiting. She belongs
to places, wild places. Hurricanes don't
scare her cos she's a big lass now and
survived a few, silver strands ride her head,
manicured claws ready to slay and a heart
full of ancient echoes, blood bodies and
resistance, wilderness and not-otherness but
'this-ness'. This-ness and this creative
life.

Audre advises me | 2019 Mid-Air

ms*| over & over &
over again spoken &
verbal & made &
shared| i bruised &
believe|the risk most
i m p o r t a n t | e v e n
*understood||

Name. D Kaur YEAR TUTORS REPORT

Number of absences and times late

Form. 3Y

Absences	Late
16	1

Dalbinder is clearly a capable
pupil but she seems to lack the
self-discipline to maintain a
consistent effort in all
her subjects.

I hope
that she will learn
from her mistakes and
improve her attitude
so that she can do
herself justice.

- attention | 1983 Sheffield

Examination	%Mark.	Position	Effort Grade (A-E)
Result	4	8	E

Average Mark	No. In class set
52	8

She is now completely
out of her depth
and has not put in
the required effort.
There are frankly,
no prospects of O-level
success.

- deficit | 1985 Sheffield

I had a dream once, a horrific
interruption that still shocks me.
I lived in a tiny terraced
house in Nottingham, on
ancient battle-land, bloodied
bodies strata-fied beneath her,
genetic rememberings of a long
ago capital. A hooded shadow
burst into her bedroom with
hurricane intensity, in the
darkest darkness, an atrocious
force ripping the covers from her
bed and sucking every part of her
soul from me. It woke I. Or was
I already awake?

Foetalising in the corner,
staining the wall,
wild-eyed horror,
heart punching ribs.

It was this kind of force that stole
my imagination – a slow aching
pull of the covers. I was too
young to know any better. Folding
the hurts into her brain.

– I was haunted for years.

"What are the tyrannies you swallow day by day and attempt to make your own, until you sicken and die of them, still in silence." Audre Lorde

Dear Aunty Audre,

I swallowed innumerable tyrannies over years & years, they turned me inside out, back in again and sickened me. The sicknesses included:

depressioning
suicidaling
disassociationing
anxietying
scatterationing
regretfulling
fear-fulling
racialising
the dead-end day jobbing
'The Professional Careering'
stresssssssing
presssssurising
shagginging
the manyfathomed depthness of knowing the path that i didn't following
un-believing-in-myselfnessing
confidencelessnessing
unremitting escape pathings - here!

no, here! no, here! no hearing
deep burying of boneings
silencing
destroying

They have to go somewhere, all these swallowings.
They crawled under my skin,
then onto the surface.

They snapped my synapses and
flicked my neurotransmitters.

They hardwired my circuitry into
fractured functioning.
Amygdalinglingling.

Nothing.
Something.

Swallowing men swallowing me.
Spending life. Expending.

Exhaling.
But I didn't die Aunty.
And I haven't stayed silent.

it just took a long time to wake up|

– hyperactivity

i knew || 2016

grief is a feral awakening, dragging you into an under-other-world whether you want to go there or not | it is getting your clitoris trapped in a slamming door | & the rest of the world feels slow motion and irrelevant | you are cracked open enough to find the wild creature that has been sitting waiting quietly inside of you for 2 and a half decades | saying - i knew you would come back and find me one day |

Jadoo stirred into a final breath
a fragrant cloud blown into my palm
i can hear you now
Left-handed practice begins.
Only i get to name I||

SS Kular 1/1/29 – 17/2/16

After you left | 2017

For years I was a carbon
copy shadow. The wolf at the door
scratched when the veil
was thin. Something
snuck in. I wrote but i
didn't know what to write. I
wrote but i didn't know what to
write. i wrote.

***

i visited Stanage Edge, day after night
after day, searching for bones. i
had to get lost, scramble over
rocks, scratch the midge lumps
on peppered calves until i could fit no more
skin under my nails. nitnem
simran kirtan waheguru satnam
waheguru. guru.
last breath blown into left
palm, duende.

2019 | Orkney

Lightning flashes. i am a brilliant

strikening breaking silence.

A wild shapeshiftering.

Tell me new stories – flood

the urban lies. i prefer

to be formed elemental –

stand earth-stacked,

wind-hacked, salt-slapped

with the Old Wo-man of Hoy.

Then: at Dingiehowies the gale blew my bones back into the shape of who i always knew I was. Am. Now i create I - from Eastern wind etching my face, firewood cracking in night woods under blood moon, from a cunctipotent pulse rolling around the Milky Way, wearing stone circles for bracelets, kissing a great owl at dawn, dreaming with night sky ink pumped through henna'd barrel.

Ms. Understood)

Dec 2019 | Election

Amygdala yanks invisible black
plait tethering me
to a formation of
flashback.
Is it 1983?
Again?

– disorder?

This moment i find myself in.
Pulled back Right.
Identity is formed in the historical
context within which i exist.

Just try it.
Just you dare try and pull me Right
back. Last breath blown into Left
palm. i am my ancestors
& survived.

i am a velocity
of contexts & confusions
& subterfuges.
i am the thin place
– the veil.
i am the Ghost.

Null to Nakodar to
Sheffield to Sutlej
and back again.
Left-handed practice begins.
i cannot write Right.

Other-wired

/i walk edges,

partitions, crumbled

gritstone spines,

a steel halo rings my

soul/ made by wild

gods & stolen wishes.

This is what i choose.

This is my definition.

This is how i name myself I.

- Dalbinder Kaur Kular

Epilogue

After a traumatic event post traumatic growth occurs and may have fuelled my creativity. Creativity heals trauma. Almost, I would argue.

Prolonged trauma shrinks the hippocampus and enlarges the amygdala. This can lead to disassociation - neuroprotective function. Ambient stress affects the structure of the brain, its function and gene expression. Creating neurovulnerability.

Books and words bounced against my amygdala for two and a half decades. I was so traumatised it was too much to even read. Or write. I had buried myself so deep, folded myself so cleverly into myself that I was almost lost. Damned to the underground. Juggling the deathwish. But it was there always. I was writing under my skin. Sometimes so hard that I had to stop but I failed to listen. To heal this trauma I needed a big one, ECT – electro-creative-therapy – to shock me awake.

And the funny thing is. I was always writing to cope. To heal. To survive. It's where I began when I wrote about snow-men. Only to begin again now. In the opening scenes of Sholay, the 1970's Bollywood classic, dacouts on horseback are chasing a steam train, trying to bring it to a halt and raid it. Thakur, the police inspector, is transporting two notorious bandits, Veeru (Dhamendra) and Jaidev (the legend that is Amitabh Bachman), handcuffed to each other. Persuading Thakur that they could fight off the entire gun Thakur splits their cuffed hands with a single bullet. Veeru and Jaidev get to work, hand-fighting the bandits, shovelling hot coal into the engine to make it go faster, shooting bandits from horses. Bandit after Bandit goes down. Watching it feels like everyone of those naysayers and internal demons that inhabit me is being shot dead. I am shouting out loud; Veeru...Jaidev! In my imagination I am shooting each dacout with night ink through a henna'd barrel. It is December

22nd 2019. The last time I saw this film was in 1974, Attercliffe, Sheffield – munching Bombay mix and sucking the dregs of Coca Cola through a paper straw from the bottom of a glass bottle.

It has been a long journey. I made it home.

I kept that last breath in my pocket. One day, I will pass it on.

Acknowledgments

This work would not exist if it were not for the dreams of my ancestors ~ believers of freedom & possibilities. With much gratitude & thanks for all those who have walked, prayered & survived before me. I remember you.

For my late mother Rishpal Kaur & my late father Sowaran Singh Kular ~ for all your prayers, blessings & wisdom. I miss you.

With enormous gratitude to Fiona Hamilton, Foluke Taylor, Graham Hartill & Seth Mehl for your unwavering belief in me & encouragement.

Special thanks to Claire Williamson for care-full guidance, inspiration & editing.

Thank you to Natalie Leyland for painting my words alive & to all my friends who read this work & who have supported me all the way.

Thank you to all the poets & authors & mystics who have inspired & infused my wor(l)ds from Audre Lorde to Baba Farid.

Lastly, Mado Yasmin Khan ~ this one is for you.

p.5:

"…the decision to define ourselves, name ourselves, and speak for ourselves, instead of being defined and spoken for by others." The Transformation of Silence into Language and Action, Sister Outsider, Penguin Random House. © 1984 by Audre Lorde.

p.17:

"What are the tyrannies you swallow day by day and attempt to make your own, until you sicken and die of them, still in silence." The Transformation of Silence into Language and Action, Sister Outsider, Penguin Random House. © 1984 by Audre Lorde.

Author Biography

Dal Kular is a writer and facilitator from Sheffield. From leaving school at 16 years old with 3 O-levels and being told she could never be a writer – to severe burnout, grief and loss – Dal returned to the power of words and writing in her late forties, as an act of radical self-care and healing, gaining an MSc in Therapeutic Writing. Through writing circles, co-writing spaces and Our True Nature writing workshops for women of colour – she encourages women to discover the power of their own voices. Her essays have been shortlisted for Wasafiri New Writing Prize and Class Action Nature Writing Prize. She is currently working on a memoir about her mother, grief and nature supported by Arts Council funding. She is most often found roaming the Peak District in her tiny brown van, Muddy. You can find out more at www.dalkular.com.

Fly on the Wall Press

A publisher with a conscience.

Publishing high quality anthologies, novels, short stories and poetry on pressing issues, from exceptional writers around the globe. Founded in 2018 by founding editor, Isabelle Kenyon.

Some other publications:

The Woman With An Owl Tattoo by Anne Walsh Donnelly

The Prettyboys of Gangster Town by Martin Grey

The Sound of the Earth Singing to Herself by Ricky Ray

Inherent by Lucia Orellana Damacela

Medusa Retold by Sarah Wallis

Pigskin by David Hartley

We Are All Somebody

Aftereffects by Jiye Lee

Someone Is Missing Me by Tina Tamsho-Thomas

*Odd as F*ck by Anne Walsh Donnelly*

Muscle and Mouth by Louise Finnigan

Modern Medicine by Lucy Hurst

These Mothers of Gods by Rachel Bower

Sin Is Due To Open In A Room Above Kitty's by Morag Anderson

Fauna by David Hartley

How To Bring Him Back by Clare HM

No One Has Any Intention of Building A Wall by Ruth Brandt

The House with Two Letter-Boxes by Janet H Swinney

Snapshots of the Apocalypse by Katy Wimhurst

A Dedication to Drowning by Maeve McKenna

In Conversation with... Literary Editors

Of Myths and Mothers

Warriors by Sundra Lawrence

Social Media:
@fly_press (Twitter)
@flyonthewall_poetry (Instagram)
@flyonthewallpress (Facebook)
www.flyonthewallpress.co.uk